The Cherokee

People, Culture, and History

by Twila M. Barnes

CAPSTONE PRESS
a capstone imprint

For my grandchildren—Noah, Penny, Ricky, and Gabriel

AUTHOR ACKNOWLEDGMENTS

No one does this work all on their own, especially in Cherokee contexts. I would like to say a special thank you to Andrea L. Rogers for opening the door, stepping aside, and then pushing me through it because she saw potential in me that I didn't see in myself. My dad, the late Bennie McCown, also deserves recognition, because without him there, always defending my right to grow into the Cherokee woman that I am today, I never could have authored this book. I would also like to express my gratitude to Trent Hickman, Daniel Heath Justice, Michael Wren, David Keith Hampton, Julie Reed, Rose Stremlau, Anita Finger-Smith, Tressie Neely, Traci Sorell, and Bryan Shade for their guidance, insight, and support in this book.

In Memory

MARIAH LEIGHANNE MURRELL
July 29, 1994 – April 5, 2021
Cherokee Nation

TREY ALLEN GLASS
September 7, 2004 – April 5, 2024
United Keetoowah Band

Published by Capstone Press, an imprint of Capstone
1710 Roe Crest Drive, North Mankato, Minnesota 56003
capstonepub.com

Library of Congress Cataloging-in-Publication Data is available on the Library of Congress website.

ISBN: 9798875208263 (hardcover)
ISBN: 9798875208218 (paperback)
ISBN: 9798875208225 (ebook PDF)

Summary: The traditions, culture, and history of the Cherokee people are showcased through engaging text, sidebars, activities, maps, and more.

Editorial Credits
Editor: Erika L. Shores; Designer: Heidi Thompson; Media Researcher: Jo Miller; Production Specialist: Tori Abraham

Image Credits
Alamy: Danita Delimont, 29, David Lyons, 21, Don Klumpp, 20; Associated Press: Paul Morigi/ Smithsonian National Museum of the American Indian, 13 (top); Bridgeman Images: © Courtesy, American Antiquarian Society; Getty Images: ilbusca, 9, MPI, 11; Library of Congress: Prints and Photographs Division, 13 (bottom right); Newscom: Miguel Juarez Lugo/ZUMA Press, 16, Picture History, 12, Robin Rayne/ZUMA Press Wire, 27; Photo Courtesy Twila Barnes, cover; Shutterstock: Bardocz Peter, 4, Hintau Aliaksei, 19 (frog), Jeaniepie, 19 (sun), MaraZe, 23, Pyty, 5, RaksyBH, 14, Runrun2 (brush stroke), back cover, spine, 1, Sergey Dudikov, 22, Vineyard Perspective, 7, 25; Superstock: piemags/PL Photography Limited, 18; Wikimedia: Official White House Photo/Pete Souza, 28

Printed in the United States 6504

TABLE OF CONTENTS

Words in **bold** are in the glossary.

ABOUT THE CHEROKEE

Cherokee Homeland

The Cherokee people lived in North America for thousands of years before their first recorded contact with Europeans. In 1540, the Cherokee Nation included most of what is today West Virginia, Virginia, North Carolina, South Carolina, Kentucky, Tennessee, Georgia, and Alabama.

Cherokee Culture

Cherokee culture was based on hunting, trading, and farming. People lived in homes made of wooden frames, covered with vines or saplings. Cherokee towns had their own leaders, governments, town houses, and councils.

What is culture?

The beliefs and values of a group of people make up their culture. Clothing, tools, and artifacts of a people are also a part of culture. Just like all cultures, Cherokee culture has changed and continues to change over time.

Today the historical Cherokee Nation is divided into three sovereign tribal governments.

THE CHEROKEE NATION
THE UNITED KEETOOWAH BAND OF CHEROKEE INDIANS
THE EASTERN BAND OF CHEROKEE INDIANS

What is a sovereign tribal government?

- A government separate from the U.S. government
- Determines who can be enrolled citizens
- Preserves its own culture
- Makes and enforces its own laws

Where are the Cherokee tribal governments located?

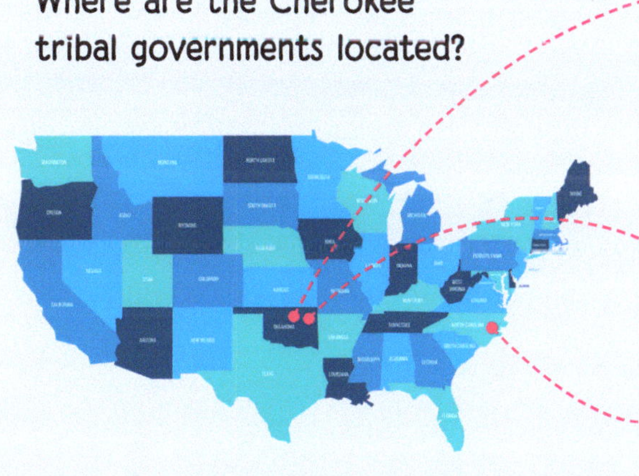

THE CHEROKEE NATION

- Northeastern Oklahoma
- More than 450,000 enrolled citizens worldwide

THE UNITED KEETOOWAH BAND

- Northeastern Oklahoma
- More than 14,300 enrolled citizens

THE EASTERN BAND

- North Carolina on their own purchased land, the Qualla Boundary
- More than 16,300 enrolled citizens

CHEROKEE CELEBRATIONS

The three Cherokee tribes have their own annual celebrations. These events celebrate Cherokee **heritage**. Events bring together families and friends.

Each September, citizens of the Cherokee Nation celebrate the Cherokee National Holiday. People come together to hear speeches, play games, and watch sporting events. Families gather. This holiday has been celebrated since 1953. It marks the signing of the 1839 **Constitution** of the Cherokee Nation.

The United Keetoowah Band has its celebration the first weekend in October. It marks the official vote in 1950 to approve their constitution.

The Eastern Band has a fall festival to celebrate the time of the Green Corn Ceremony. This traditional celebration gives thanks for the corn harvest. It is also a time of forgiveness among one another.

Cherokee ambassadors ride on a float during the Cherokee National Holiday parade.

THE NATION'S HISTORY

Before the arrival of Europeans, the Cherokee Nation was made up of many tribal towns. Together, they formed the entire Cherokee Nation. In 1785, leaders of the Cherokee Nation and the newly formed United States met and signed their first **treaty**. Many treaties followed. The Cherokee Nation often had to give up land in exchange for peace with the U.S. government.

By 1790, about 1,000 Cherokees had moved west of the Mississippi River. They did this to escape the growing population of **colonizers** moving into the area. The Cherokees who moved were called Old Settlers. They had their own government, apart from the Cherokee Nation. They lived in scattered areas west of the Mississippi River, eventually settling in a place called Indian Territory.

From 1817 to 1819, the Cherokee Nation made treaties with the U.S. government that encouraged more Cherokees to move west and join the Old Settlers. Those treaties also allowed some Cherokees in North Carolina to become "citizen Indians" of that state. They were no longer part of the main body of Cherokees.

Cherokees built their homes near one another in small towns.

After the United States formed into a country, some Cherokees began living like their American counterparts. They dressed like Americans. They sometimes married Americans. They even started their own newspaper using both the Cherokee and English languages. They thought if they lived like Americans, they would not have to give up more land.

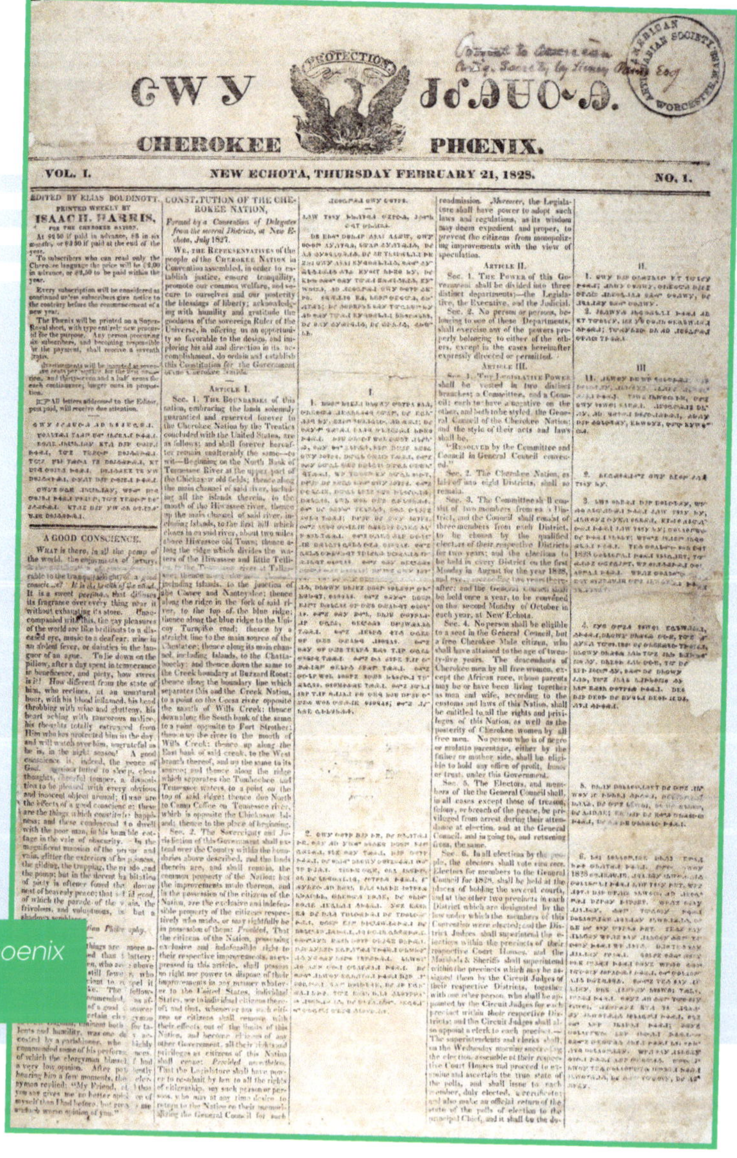

PROTECTION

ᏣᎳᎩ ᏧᎴᎯᏌᏅᎯ.

CHEROKEE PHOENIX.

VOL. I. NEW ECHOTA, THURSDAY FEBRUARY 21, 1828. NO. 1.

EDITED BY ELIAS BOUDINOTT.
PRINTED WEEKLY BY
ISAAC H. HARRIS,
FOR THE CHEROKEE NATION.

At $2 50 if paid in advance, $3 in six months, or $3 50 if paid at the end of the year.

To subscribers who can read only the Cherokee language the price will be $2,00 in advance, or $2,50 to be paid within the year.

Every subscription will be considered as continued unless subscribers give notice to the contrary before the commencement of a new year.

The Phoenix will be printed on a Super-Royal sheet, with type entirely new procured for the purpose. Any person procuring six subscribers, and becoming responsible for the payment, shall receive a seventh gratis.

Advertisements will be inserted at seventy-five cents per square for the first insertion, and thirty-seven and a half cents for each continuance; longer ones in proportion.

☞ All letters addressed to the Editor, post paid, will receive due attention.

A GOOD CONSCIENCE.

WHAT is there, in all the pomp of the world, the enjoyments of luxury, ... comparable to the tranquil delight of a good conscience? It is the health of the mind. It is a sweet perfume, that diffuses its fragrance over every thing near it without exhausting its store. ...

CONSTITUTION OF THE CHEROKEE NATION,

Formed by a Convention of Delegates from the several Districts, at New Echota, July 1827.

WE, THE REPRESENTATIVES of the people of the CHEROKEE NATION in Convention assembled, in order to establish justice, ensure tranquility, promote our common welfare, and secure to ourselves and our posterity the blessings of liberty; acknowledging with humility and gratitude the goodness of the sovereign Ruler of the Universe, in offering us an opportunity so favorable to the design, and imploring his aid and direction in its accomplishment, do ordain and establish this Constitution for the Government of the Cherokee Nation.

ARTICLE I.

Sec. 1. THE BOUNDARIES of this nation, embracing the lands solemnly guarantied and reserved forever to the Cherokee Nation by the Treaties concluded with the United States, are as follows; and shall forever hereafter remain unalterably the same—to wit—Beginning on the North Bank of Tennessee River at the upper part of the Chickasaw old fields; thence along the main channel of said river, including all the islands therein, to the mouth of the Hiwassee river, thence up the main channel of said river, including Islands, to the first hill which closes in on said river, about two miles above Hiwassee old Town; thence along the ridge which divides the waters of the Hiwassee and little Tellico, ... including islands, to the junction of the Conasauga and Nantayalee; thence along the ridge in the fork of said river, to the top of the blue ridge; thence along the blue ridge to the Unicoy Turnpike road; ...

...

readmission. *Moreover*, the Legislature shall have power to adopt such laws and regulations, as its wisdom may deem expedient and proper, to *prevent the citizens from monopolizing* improvements with the view of speculation.

ARTICLE II.

Sec. 1. THE POWER of this Government shall be divided into three distinct departments;—the Legislative, the Executive, and the Judicial.

Sec. 2. No person or persons, belonging to one of these Departments, shall exercise any of the powers properly belonging to either of the others, except in the cases hereinafter expressly directed or permitted.

ARTICLE III.

Sec. 1. THE LEGISLATIVE POWER shall be vested in two distinct branches; a Committee, and a Council; each to have a negative on the other, and both to be styled the General Council of the Cherokee Nation; and the style of their acts and laws shall be,

"RESOLVED by the Committee and Council in General Council convened."

Sec. 2. The Cherokee Nation, as laid off into eight Districts, shall so remain.

Sec. 3. The Committee shall consist of two members from each District, and the Council shall consist of three members from each District, to be chosen by the qualified electors of their respective Districts for two years; and the elections to be held in every District on the first Monday in August for the year 1828, and every succeeding two years thereafter; and the General Council shall be held once a year, to be convened on the second Monday of October in each year, at New Echota.

Sec. 4. No person shall be eligible to a seat in the General Council, but a free Cherokee Male citizen, who shall have attained to the age of twenty-five years. ...

Cherokee Phoenix newspaper

In 1814, Cherokee Nation warriors helped U.S. General Andrew Jackson. They defeated members of the Muscogee Creek Nation at the Battle of Horseshoe Bend. A Cherokee saved Jackson's life during the battle.

Fourteen years later, Jackson became the U.S. president. But he was no longer a friend to Cherokees. He wanted the U.S. Congress to pass the Indian Removal Act of 1830. This would force tribes living in the southeast, including the Cherokee, to give up their national land and move west of the Mississippi River.

Sequoyah

Cherokee leader Sequoyah created a system of writing for the Cherokee language. He made a syllabary, the use of symbols for syllables in a language. It represented each sound in the Cherokee oral language. His syllabary was used to write legal documents. It was used to write the *Cherokee Phoenix*, the first Native American newspaper. Sequoyah helped create the 1839 Constitution of the Cherokee Nation.

Cherokees did not want to leave their homeland. They took legal action against moving. They won in the U.S. Supreme Court. But President Jackson refused to follow the ruling of the court.

In 1835, a Cherokee group decided to **negotiate** with the United States. Today, the group is known as "the Treaty Party." The Treaty Party had not been elected by the Cherokee people. They had no authority to act on behalf of the Cherokee government. But the group signed the Treaty of New Echota.

In the treaty, they agreed the Cherokee Nation would give up its homeland and move to Indian Territory with the Old Settlers. Even though the treaty was not legal, it led to the forced removal of the Cherokee people from their homeland.

The U.S. military arrested Cherokees. They were held in crowded camps until being moved to Indian Territory. Nearly 4,000 Cherokees died during this time. Today this forced removal is better known as the Cherokee Trail of Tears.

More than 16,000 Cherokees were forced to leave their homelands during the Trail of Tears.

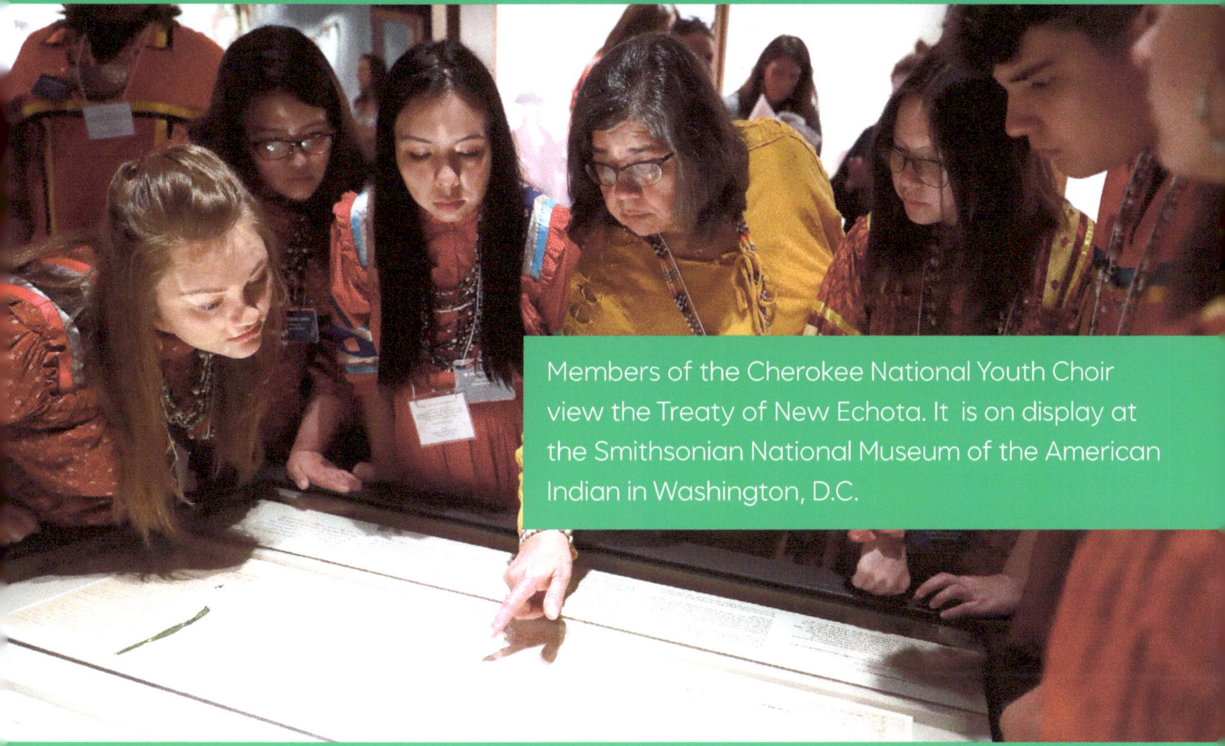

Members of the Cherokee National Youth Choir view the Treaty of New Echota. It is on display at the Smithsonian National Museum of the American Indian in Washington, D.C.

Chief John Ross

Chief John Ross was principal chief of the Cherokee Nation from 1828 to 1866. Ross led the Cherokee people through the most difficult times in Cherokee history. These events included the forced removal of his people from their homeland in 1838 to 1839 and the U.S. Civil War that divided the Cherokee Nation. He died in Washington, D.C., in 1866 while trying to negotiate another treaty with the United States.

In the late 1800s, the U.S. government wanted to make Oklahoma a state. To do that, it had to put an end to the governments and nations in Indian Territory. This included the Cherokee Nation.

Dissolving their nation would leave Cherokees without citizenship, so they would be given citizenship in the United States. Cherokees who followed the old ways, called Nighthawks, were against the dissolution of their nation.

The Nighthawks refused to report to the Dawes Commission. This U.S. government group was taking applications for a final roll. Despite stories claiming some Cherokees were never listed, all living Nighthawks and Cherokee Nation citizens were put on this roll. If a Cherokee refused to enroll, informants gave their information. The Dawes Commission also checked old rolls to ensure all Cherokees had been included on the Final Dawes Rolls.

The intent of the U.S. government was to end the Cherokee Nation. The Final Dawes Rolls was supposed to be the last list of Cherokee Nation citizens, ever. However, the passage of a 1906 act by the U.S. Congress preserved the tribal nations of the Cherokees and four other tribes.

Timeline

1540	First European contact
1785	Treaty of Hopewell is signed.
1814	The Battle of Horseshoe Bend
1817-1819	Old Settler and "Citizen Indians" treaties
1821	Sequoyah introduces his syllabary.
1828	*Cherokee Phoenix* becomes the first Native American newspaper.
1830	The Indian Removal Act
1832	U.S. Supreme Court rules the Cherokee Nation is a sovereign nation.
1835	The Treaty of New Echota is signed.
1838-1839	The Trail of Tears
1839	The Old Settler and Emigrant Cherokees reunite under the 1839 Constitution.
1863	Cherokee Emancipation Proclamation
1866	Treaty of 1866 and the adoption of Cherokee Freedmen
1887	The Dawes Act
1902-1906	The Final Dawes Rolls
1907	Oklahoma becomes a state.
1924-1929	Baker Roll, Eastern Cherokee
1950	Federal recognition for the United Keetoowah Band of Cherokee Indians
1975	The Cherokee Nation adopts a new constitution.
1985	Wilma Mankiller becomes Cherokee Nation principal chief.
2017	Cherokee Freedmen descendants win their court battle.
2019 and 2023	Cherokee Nation Principal Chief Chuck Hoskin Jr. names Kimberly Teehee as the Delegate-designate to the U.S. House of Representatives.

CHEROKEE CULTURE

Cherokees celebrate and honor their heritage in many ways. One important way is knowing which clan they might belong to. The Cherokee have seven clans. Those clans are Wolf, Deer, Bird, Blue, Paint, Wild Potato, and Long Hair.

The Cherokee clan system is **matrilineal**. A Cherokee child belongs to their mother's clan. Only the Cherokee mother can pass her clan to her child. A Cherokee man cannot pass his clan to his children.

The role of clans has changed in Cherokee culture over time. Some families are clan-less because their mother or a grandmother was not Cherokee. Those families became Cherokee through their father or a grandfather, so they have no clan. Despite this, people who know their clans treasure it as an important aspect of being Cherokee.

Which clan a child belongs to is determined by their mother.

The Cherokee Language

Today, the Cherokee language is highly endangered, or at risk of disappearing. Its speakers are dying or speaking other languages instead of Cherokee. Citizens work to preserve their language.

The U.S. government played a large part in the loss of the Cherokee language. Cherokee children were taken and placed in **boarding schools** up until the 1960s. Children were not allowed to speak their language in these schools. To protect children from abuse at boarding schools, many Cherokee parents stopped speaking Cherokee to their children.

Practice saying and writing these Cherokee words:

edoda (eh-doe-da)—father

eduda (eh-due-da)—grandfather

elisi (eh-lee-see)—grandmother

etsi (eh-chee)—mother

goweli (go-whey-lee)—book

osda (oh-s-da)—good

osiyo (oh-see-yo)—hello

sidanelv (see-dah-nay-luh)—family

unalii (u-na-lee-ee)—friend

wado (wa-doe)—thank you

CHEROKEE CLOTHING

Cherokees of all ages often wear traditional clothing at important events. But the traditional clothing is not required to be worn. The tear dress is the official tribal clothing for women. "Tear" describes the way the fabric is ripped or torn to make the dress. It is in the style of dress worn at the time of the Trail of Tears.

The ribbon shirt is a popular shirt among Cherokee men. It is a style worn by men from many tribes. It has ribbons on both the front and the back of the shirt. The ruffle at the cuff and the length of the ribbons sets the Cherokee men's ribbon shirt apart from other tribes.

Cherokees wear pucker-toe moccasins. This style is made from one piece of leather that is gathered at the toe. The ankle side flaps are sometimes decorated with beads.

Members of the Cherokee National Youth Choir wear tear dresses and ribbon shirts when they perform.

A Giant Frog that Swallows the Sun

This Cherokee story came about because of an eclipse. An eclipse occurs when the moon passes between the earth and the sun, briefly blocking the sun.

A giant hungry frog exists that sometimes comes out and swallows the sun. When this happens, it gets dark and cold. Sometimes the frog swallows the moon instead of the sun.

The Cherokees hate the giant frog. When they see it is coming, the men make loud noises, bang drums, or shake turtle rattles. The women beat pots and pans together. This is to scare the giant frog away from swallowing the sun. The sun always shines again.

BASKET WEAVING

Basket weaving is a Cherokee art form going back thousands of years. Traditionally, the practice was passed down from mother to daughter. Today, the skill is taught through classes offered by a Cherokee tribe or through the basket weavers themselves.

Basket makers gather local materials to weave their baskets. They commonly use honeysuckle, buckbrush, and river cane. They also use walnut and bloodroot to dye their reed, vine, or river cane before it is woven into items.

Cherokee basket weaving has two methods: single and double weave. A double weave basket has two layers. One layer is inside of the other. The type of basket weave is determined by how the item will be used. Mats and rugs might have a single weave. Baskets used to carry or store things would be a double weave.

Paper Weaving Craft

Practice weaving by trying this simple paper craft.

1. Cut construction paper along the long side into 1-inch-wide strips, set aside.
2. Fold another piece of construction paper in half, long sides together.
3. At the fold, make 3-inch-long cuts about 1 inch apart.
4. Unfold the paper
5. Weave one strip of construction paper over and under the cuts until filling the length of paper.
6. Weave another strip over and under the cuts, but opposite of the weave from before.
7. Continue weaving, alternating over and under, until the cuts are filled in.
8. Trim ends of the strips and tape down to hold in place.

A member of the Eastern Band of Cherokee weaves a basket.

A TRADITIONAL FOOD

A much-loved dish enjoyed by Cherokees is called "wild onions and eggs." In spring, Cherokee families gather to search for wild onions. Grandparents often take grandchildren to "secret" locations. These are spots where they were taken by their grandparents when they were children. Year after year, the family returns to dig up the wild onions growing there.

Once gathered, the wild onions are washed, trimmed, and cooked. Cherokees prepare wild onions one of two ways. Some families cook the onions in boiling water until tender. Then they add beaten raw eggs and let it cook. Other families cook the onions in bacon grease until tender, then add beaten eggs, and cook the mixture until the eggs are done.

Wild onions can be found in meadows, forests, and fields.

A Cherokee Recipe

Long ago, this recipe was made with juice from wild grapes. Today, Cherokees often use grape juice from the grocery store. This recipe involves boiling liquid. An adult helper is required.

GRAPE DUMPLINGS

Ingredients

- 2 cups of self-rising flour
- ½ cup of sugar
- 1½ cups of milk or water
- 5¾–6 cups of grape juice

Instructions

1. Mix flour and sugar together.
2. Stir in milk or water.
3. Press dough on to lightly floured surface until thin.
4. Cut into 1x1-inch pieces.
5. Pour grape juice into pan and bring to a boil.
6. Drop 1-inch pieces into boiling grape juice and cook for 15 minutes, stirring as needed.

STICKBALL

A favorite sport among Cherokees is stickball. It is like the game lacrosse. Historically, as boys grew into teenagers, they began to play stickball. Cherokees viewed this sport as a rite of passage. It was a way for boys to learn skills used in war.

Each player carried two wooden sticks. Each stick had a webbed scoop on the end. The ball was passed from player to player. Games lasted for hours. They were often violent.

Today, Cherokees still play stickball. They often hold tournaments during celebrations or other big events. Women compete alongside men. The game is not violent like it was in the past, but players still compete fiercely.

Stickball players demonstrate how the game is played during a parade.

DANCES

Today, modern powwows are held across North America. The dancing has roots in the warrior societies of Plains tribes but has turned into a modern-day celebration of many tribes. Powwows are not culturally Cherokee. But the practice has been adopted at the Cherokee National Holiday as a homecoming celebration. It's also a way to show friendship with other tribes. The Eastern Band hosts a Fourth of July powwow for the same reasons.

Traditional Cherokees have Stomp Dances, or Stomps. These dances are both social and spiritual gatherings. Stomps are held at ceremonial places called Stomp Grounds. Unlike powwows where anyone can attend and watch, Stomps are not public events. One must be invited to attend a Stomp Dance if they are not a member of the Stomp Ground.

Children from the Eastern Band of Cherokee play during a powwow.

RECONNECTING

Many Native Americans, including Cherokees, moved from their tribal lands to cities during the 1950s. This was part of a policy by the U.S. government to encourage tribal members to give up their culture. Because of this, many Cherokees and their families became disconnected, or lost touch with one another and their heritage.

Kimberly Teehee

Kimberly Teehee is an attorney, politician, and activist. She grew up in Claremore, Oklahoma, and is a fluent speaker of the Cherokee language. She was the Senior Policy Adviser for Native American Affairs under the Obama Administration from 2009 to 2012. Teehee is the first Cherokee Nation Delegate-designate to the U.S. House of Representatives, a right promised in the Treaties of Hopewell and New Echota. As of 2024, Teehee had not been seated by Congress. The U.S. government remained unsure if and how they should enact this treaty obligation.

Learning from Elders is important to keeping the Cherokee culture alive.

Today, relocated Cherokees might return to reconnect with Cherokees living on tribal land. They are often asked, "Who are your people?" The answer is the last name of one's Cherokee family along with the name of the Cherokee community the family came from. This conversation helps Cherokees find out how they are connected to one another. For this same reason, Cherokees often research their family's **genealogy**. They want to know who their ancestors were and discover new relatives. In this way, Cherokee culture, past and present, is brought together.

Glossary

boarding school (BOR-ding SKOOL)—a place where students live while they are going to school at the same time

colonizer (KAH-luh-nye-zur)—a nation or government that claims a territory other than its own

constitution (kahn-stuh-TOO-shuhn)—the system of laws that state the rights of the people and the powers of the government

genealogy (JEE-nee-ah-luh-gee)—the study of family lines of ancestors

heritage (HER-uh-tij)—history and traditions handed down from the past

matrilineal (mat-truh-LIN-ee-uhl)—following a person's descent through the mother's family line

negotiate (ni-GOH-shee-ate)—to handle a matter through discussion in order to come to an agreement

treaty (TREE-tee)—a written agreement between two groups

Read More

Sorell, Traci. *We Are Grateful: Otsaliheliga: Seasons.* Watertown, MA: Charlesbridge, 2024.

Sorell, Traci. *We Are Still Here!: Native American Truths Everyone Should Know*. Watertown, MA: Charlesbridge, 2021.

Wagnon, Brad. *Cherokee: The People and Nation.* Collingwood, ON: Beech Street Books, 2024.

Internet Sites

Anadisgoi
anadisgoi.com/index.php/culture

Cherokee Coloring Sheets
language.cherokee.org/learning-materials/cherokee-coloring-sheets/

Visit Cherokee
visitcherokeenc.com/culture/

Index

About the Author

Twila M. Barnes is a homeschooling grandma who is passionate about Cherokee culture, history, and education. She's raising the three oldest children of her deceased daughter and giving them a blended Cherokee American education. She's a professional genealogist who specializes in Cherokee lineages and history with more than 20 years of experience. She grew up in Windsor, Missouri, and earned her bachelor's degree at the University of Central Missouri. She's a citizen of the Cherokee Nation and a descendant of the United Keetoowah Band of Cherokee Indians. She currently lives in southern Missouri with her family and three dogs.